Rio Grande in the Rockies
A Contemporary Glimpse

By Ronald C. Hill

Colorado Railroad Museum

Acknowledgments

The author wishes to express his sincere appreciation to F. Hol Wagner, Jr., editor of the *Burlington Northern Annual,* for his superb editorial and layout work; to Howard L. Fogg, Ed Fulcomer, and Ross B. Grenard for providing excellent photographs to make the coverage more complete; and to Alexis McKinney, William C. Jones, Charles Albi, and Timothy S. Isaac for invaluable service, assistance, and encouragement.

COVER: The Fast Ford train speeds along the eastern approach to Tennessee Pass near the old station of Keeldar under the watchful gaze of 14,431-foot Mt. Elbert, highest peak in the Colorado Rockies. (2/13/76)

TITLE PAGE: On a cold, dry winter morning, the *Rio Grande Zephyr* climbs steadily toward tunnel #1, just below Plainview. (12/18/76)

All photographs are by the author except where otherwise credited.

Library of Congress Card Number 77-8187
ISBN 0-918 654-04-1

Published by the Colorado Railroad Historical Foundation, Inc.
Colorado Railroad Museum
P. O. Box 10
Golden, Colorado 80401

Printed and bound in the United States of America by
Johnson Publishing Company
Boulder, Colorado

Typography by
Obenchain Printing Company
Denver, Colorado

Introduction

Ron Hill is a Denver lawyer whose leisure time is spent in anything-but-leisurely pursuit of his talent as a photographer and his love and respect for railroads.

Lawyer Hill is a romanticist about trains, but he also is a realist. He fulfills his affections with the past as a trustee of the Colorado Railroad Historical Foundation and Museum at Golden, Colorado. In this book he pays noteworthy tribute to the surviving and still-striving passenger trains; but the strength of his publication comes from his action photographs of the hard-working, efficient diesel-powered freight trains that are the basic haulers of cross-country commerce.

Author Hill's four titled sections of *Rio Grande in the Rockies*, with some 80 photographs taken since 1960, bring us through the recent past of the Denver & Rio Grande Western Railroad into its present.

"The Joint Line" covers the railroad along the original route of the Rio Grande, now more important than ever in the new energy-conscious West.

"Tennessee Pass" and "The Moffat Road" have provided ideal subjects for modern mountain railroad pictures — provided, indeed, the photographer has the skill, energy, and sometimes the patience, to catch the train at the right place and moment, as Ron Hill has.

"Passenger Service" recalls the trains that today's motoring, flying public once used to travel scenic Colorado — the *Royal Gorge,* the *Prospector,* the *Yampa Valley,* and the *California Zephyr*. It depicts the two remaining D&RGW passenger trains — the *Rio Grande Zephyr* and the Winter Park *Ski Train*.

Ron Hill's pictures are strong reminders of the present vitality of railroading as well as pleasant reflections upon a yesterday that all but the youngest among us remember well.

G. B. Aydelott
Chairman, Denver & Rio Grande Western Railroad

The Joint Line

The Denver & Rio Grande Railway was organized in 1870 as a narrow gauge north-south railroad projected to run from Denver to the Mexican border. Later considerations confined the fledgling railroad to a much smaller geographic area. Construction began in 1871, and the slim gauge track reached Colorado Springs that October. Tracklayers got as far as Pueblo by June 15, 1872, but within a few years it was obvious that a narrow gauge main line would not suffice in the face of increasing railroad activity in Colorado. To meet standard gauge competition, the Rio Grande hastily converted its line between Denver and Pueblo to standard gauge during 1881. So hurried was this project that a third rail was spiked to longer ties inserted into the narrow gauge track. By that method narrow gauge traffic was not seriously disrupted.

In the meantime, the Atchison, Topeka & Santa Fe had pushed its Colorado trackage from Rocky Ford to Pueblo in 1876. The Santa Fe then built westward over Raton Pass and later elected also to extend its line north to Denver. The new Santa Fe line roughly paralleled that of the Rio Grande and reached Denver in 1887. It was formally opened for operation on January 1, 1888.

Early in 1899 the Santa Fe and the Colorado & Southern Railway entered into an agreement whereby the C&S was permitted to use the AT&SF tracks between South Denver and Pueblo. A more significant development occurred in 1918 when the Rio Grande and Santa Fe entered into a joint operating agreement for the trackage between South Denver and Bragdon, ten miles north of Pueblo. During 1918 connecting tracks between the Rio Grande and the Santa Fe lines were installed at South Denver, Sedalia, Spruce, Fountain, and Bragdon. Right-hand double-track operation commenced in October, 1918, and the Colorado & Southern also enjoyed trackage rights as a tenant of the AT&SF. Thus, the original Rio Grande main line became a part of what was familiarly known as the "Joint Line."

In 1974, after several years of negotiations, the Santa Fe finally acceded to demands that it remove its line through Colorado Springs, where there were many grade crossings. Apparently annoyed by the presence of the railroad, the City of Colorado Springs had even passed a municipal ordinance prohibiting trains from whistling within the city limits. The Joint Line was single-tracked between Palmer Lake and Crews, just south of Colorado Springs. That decision may be regretted in the future as coal traffic continues to increase dramatically.

A deceptively steep grade from Denver to Palmer Lake is the major obstacle on the Joint Line. When the tonnage grows too heavy, helper locomotives are utilized by the D&RGW. Normally positioned behind the caboose, the pushers are then cut off on the fly at Palmer Lake summit. Helper engines are not found on the Santa Fe, as the Joint Line is not a helper district for that railroad. The Colorado & Southern depends upon remote-controlled slave units to boost its heavy coal trains up the hill. Ironically, the tenant C&S now hauls more traffic over the Joint Line than either of the two owners. While the C&S and AT&SF frequently combine trains and power, the D&RGW ordinarily uses no engines but its own.

The present-day Joint Line throbs with the activity of three different railroads and transports varied items such as coal, iron ore, beer and general merchandise. It is a far cry indeed from the days of the last century when diminutive Rio Grande locomotives chugged slowly back and forth between Denver and Pueblo on light narrow gauge rails. The first section of this volume views briefly the modern operation of the Denver & Rio Grande Western Railroad on its first main line. Succeeding chapters are devoted to Tennessee Pass, the Moffat Road, and passenger service.

In 1961, the D&RGW purchased three revolutionary 4,000 h.p. diesel-hydraulic locomotives from Kraus-Maffei in Germany. While they were the most powerful diesel units in the world at that time, they were plagued by a variety of mechanical problems, including cracked wheels and inadequate air intake. Eventually they were confined to the Joint Line so as never to be far away from the Denver shops. All three were sold to the Southern Pacific in 1964 and scrapped in 1968. Here #4001 is seen undergoing air intake modifications at Burnham Shops in Denver. (4/6/62)

A 3,600 h.p. SD45, now the most powerful engine on the Rio Grande roster, is on the point of a southbound freight out of Littleton. (9/6/76)

A short, fast train rolls north through Wolhurst. (2/14/76)

Occasionally tonnage headed south from Denver is so great that helper engines are required as far as Palmer Lake. This helper train is viewed as it passes through Wolhurst. (2/14/76)

A trio of SD40T-2's powers a freight headed south near Sedalia. (1/31/76)

A southbound helper train is pictured coming and going at Sedalia with SD40T-2's pulling on the front and GP40-2's pushing on the rear. (2/14/76)

Climbing through Larkspur on the grade which crests at Palmer Lake, this freight is actually operating on the AT&SF track. (12/1/74)

A heavy coal train powered by five SD40T-2's, which were acquired specifically for coal train service, approaches Palmer Lake. (12/3/76)

A train bound for Pueblo crosses the big AT&SF bridge over East Plum Creek and the old Denver-Colorado Springs highway at Larkspur. (9/6/76)

Palmer Lake is crisp and cold as this southbound train with an
assortment of motive power surmounts the grade. (11/24/74)

All is calm and quiet in Palmer Lake as a north-bound rolls along the shore of the lake which once served as an important source of water for steam locomotives. (12/3/76)

A freight curves around Palmer Lake and starts downgrade
toward Colorado Springs and Pueblo. (12/3/74)

Elephant Rock, famous early day landmark, is seen at upper left as an empty coal train pulled by four SD40T-2's growls northward into Palmer Lake. This portion of the line would ordinarily have been reserved for southbound traffic prior to the time part of the Joint Line was single-tracked in 1974. (10/25/76)

Five SD40T-2's are in charge of this coal train
from Denver as it rolls into Colorado Springs. (12/3/76)

Tennessee Pass

Plans of the infant Denver & Rio Grande Railway to reach Mexico were thwarted when the Santa Fe established its route over Raton Pass and effectively blocked southward Rio Grande expansion. Developers of the D&RG soon eyed the riches of Leadville, a booming mining town. Both the Rio Grande and the Santa Fe built frantically from Pueblo up the Arkansas River valley toward the Royal Gorge during 1878. The notorious "Royal Gorge War" resulted when the competing companies reached the deep, precipitous canyon which had sufficient room for only one rail line. Extensive sabotage and judicial battles were not conclusive, but two years later the powerful Jay Gould forced a settlement which awarded the Royal Gorge route to the Rio Grande.

Freed of its constraints in 1880, the Rio Grande narrow gauge line proceeded westward through the Royal Gorge to Malta, just below Leadville. By 1887, rails had surmounted the 10,424-foot summit of Tennessee Pass and reached Glenwood Springs, a resort town even then famed for its hot springs. In 1890 trackage between Pueblo and Grand Junction was converted to standard gauge. The widening project involved construction of an entirely new line between Malta and Red Cliff which pierced the Continental Divide through a half-mile tunnel under Tennessee Pass at an elevation of 10,239 feet. At the end of 1890, a new route to Salt Lake City was opened in conjunction with the Utah-based Rio Grande Western. Soon the Tennessee Pass line replaced narrow gauge Marshall Pass as the primary east-west route of the Rio Grande.

While the rebuilt railroad over Tennessee Pass featured easier grades and gentler curves, the pass remained an arduous challenge. A larger tunnel was bored under the pass in 1945 to accommodate bigger cars. Certainly the two most outstanding features of that line are the incredible Royal Gorge and lofty Tennessee Pass. In fact, Tennessee Pass marks the highest point now reached by any main line in North America. Helper service has been necessary on the west side of the pass since the line was first opened, and that requirement has not been eliminated by modern diesel power. During the age of steam, it was not uncommon to see three giant Mallets boosting a heavy train up the steep grade.

During World War II the Army established a winter training base at Camp Hale near Pando. Stories are rampant about soldiers on training maneuvers with orders to "capture" a train who were turned back in the face of mighty 3600-class articulateds storming up the pass. Now Camp Hale is only a memory with a few concrete foundations visible here and there, although the Army still conducts winter mountain training in the area on occasion.

Modern operations on Tennessee Pass are still an exciting spectacle. The west side of the pass boasts a 3% grade which necessitates as many as six mid-train helper engines on virtually all eastbound tonnage. In fact, the track between Minturn and Tennessee Pass is one of the few remaining regular helper districts in the United States. Eastward trains twist and turn through the impressive Eagle River Canyon outside of Minturn and then assault the steep 3% grade beginning near Red Cliff. One of the more spectacular locations for photography is found on the sweeping S-curve at Mitchell, just west of the summit. Another magnificent setting is on the east side near Keeldar, where 14,431-foot Mt. Elbert, highest peak in the Colorado Rockies, towers majestically in the background. Traffic is not heavy on that route, but the Missouri Pacific connection at Pueblo ordinarily generates at least three trains daily in each direction. And coal is already beginning to move east via Tennessee Pass. Some of the grandest scenery in Colorado is found along the Continental Divide near Tennessee Pass. There are fifty-four mountains in Colorado which equal or exceed 14,000 feet in elevation, and many of those high peaks are situated in the Sawatch Range of the Rocky Mountains near Leadville. The Rio Grande line over Tennessee Pass is truly an imposing setting for modern railroad operations.

An eastbound unit coal train speeds through Salida, once a busy division point. Now crews run from Minturn through Salida and all the way to Pueblo. (10/1/76)

In the valley of the Arkansas River, a westbound freight headed by a big SD45 grinds out of Salida en route to Salt Lake City by way of Tennessee Pass. (11/15/72)

Although this volume is primarily concerned with the Rio Grande's Colorado mainlines, the 22-mile Monarch Branch is too spectacular to be ignored. Completed as a narrow gauge line from Salida in 1883 to serve mines in the Monarch Pass region, the branch was converted to standard gauge and dieselized in 1956. Here an empty train winds slowly around the tight S-curve at Maysville on a 4.5% grade. (10/1/76)

The 4.5% grade and famed Garfield switchback of the Monarch Branch are now behind the train as it nears the Monarch Mine at the top end of the branch. (10/1/76)

Three GP40's and two GP35's hurry a hotshot westward
through Nathrop after meeting a coal train. (10/1/76)

Having conquered Tennessee Pass, an eastbound drops downgrade near Keeldar. (10/30/75)

A long train struggles eastward around the impressive
S-curve at Mitchell, just below the tunnel at the summit of
Tennessee Pass, with six helper engines working hard in
the middle of the consist. At the time Mitchell siding was
being removed. (Photo by Ed Fulcomer, 7/4/68)

One of the most beautiful settings on the D&RGW is
found at Keeldar, near Leadville. Mt. Elbert, the loftiest
mountain in Colorado at an elevation of 14,431 feet,
looms over time freight #71 as it winds toward
Tennessee Pass. (8/15/76)

With dynamic brakes howling, hotshot freight #71
swings through the big curve at Mitchell. (8/15/76)

At a location made famous years ago by the photographic
artistry of Richard H. Kindig, a freight throbs up the stiff
3% grade near the west end of the old Mitchell siding.
(8/14/76)

The Fast Ford train drops down
through Pando on its frantic run
to California. (2/13/76)

With engines arranged elephant-style, an east-
bound freight pauses at Pando to set out a car.
This was the site of Camp Hale, the World War
II Army winter training camp. (10/6/73)

The 3% eastward grade eases briefly at Pando to give this train a momentary respite. Six mid-train helper units provide desperately needed additional power for the arduous pull to the top of Tennessee Pass. (8/14/76)

Symbol freight #179, the Fast Ford train, drifts through Red Cliff deep in the Eagle River Canyon on the last leg of its run to Minturn, where a new crew will take over to continue the speedy run west. The Ford Motor Company periodically rotates this high-priority train among several western railroads. (8/14/76)

A long freight curves through the Eagle River Canyon near Red Cliff. As is customary on most eastward movements, six helper engines are located mid-train. (10/6/73)

An eastbound manifest climbs out of
Minturn on the difficult route leading to
Tennessee Pass. (8/14/76)

The helper locomotives patiently await their next assignment under the sand tower at Minturn, one of the few remaining helper stations in the western United States. (2/13/76)

An eastbound freight powered by four Burlington
GP35's rolls through Glenwood Springs on the
bank of the Colorado River. For a brief period
during 1965 and 1966, the Rio Grande and
Burlington pooled motive power between Salt
Lake City and Chicago. But since D&RGW
diesels are specially modified for the difficult
high-altitude terrain of Colorado and Utah, the
railroad prefers to keep them on their home rails.
(9/6/65)

Five shiny SD40T-2's furnish more than ample power for an empty coal train destined for the Eenrgy Mine near Hayden. (3/6/76)

The mountain ridge atop tunnel #1, near Plainview, affords a spectacular vantage point overlooking the original D&SL main line as a westbound train (right), climbs the sinuous trackage. About an hour later, an eastbound train (above), rolls downgrade from Plainview. (10/4/75)

Another view from the mountain over tunnel #1,
the first of fifty existing tunnels on the Moffat
Road, as train #67 twists its way into the Front
Range of the Colorado Rockies. (12/18/76)

A quartet of GP40's is in charge of a hotshot
climbing westward at Plainview. (7/29/76)

Snow is lingering in patches at the time of this
springtime picture of an eastbound train dropping
down through Plainview. (4/6/74)

Opposite: The dynamic brakes are howling as a
trio of SD45's heads an eastbound hotshot near
Rainbow Cut at Plainview. (11/30/74)

With engines straining, a westbound
freight growls through tunnel #22 above
Crescent. (7/3/71)

Three powerful SD40T-2 locomotives have no difficulty
surmounting the 2% grade between Tolland and East Portal. (6/7/75)

A short, fast westbound train bursts from
the confines of the Moffat Tunnel at
Winter Park. Completed in 1928, the
6.2-mile tunnel enabled the Moffat Road
to avoid the terrible rigors of crossing
the Continental Divide via 11,680-foot
Rollins Pass. (3/29/75)

First generation diesel power
awaits an assignment at Phippsburg.
(3/5/66)

Six F-7's power an eastward coal train near Phippsburg. The coal will be burned to generate electricity at the Public Service Company Cherokee plant in Denver. For many years the Rio Grande has played a key role in transporting coal to provide Denver with electricity. (Photo by Ed Fulcomer, 5/26/69)

Passenger Service

During the 1960's, an interesting array of standard gauge passenger trains was operated by the Rio Grande. One by one, the trains disappeared until only two remained: the tri-weekly *Rio Grande Zephyr* and the seasonal *Ski Train*. This chapter provides a brief view of the latter day passenger service.

Royal Gorge (trains 1 and 2). Successor to the famed *Scenic Limited,* the *Royal Gorge* was inaugurated on June 2, 1946, between Denver and Salt Lake City by way of the Royal Gorge and Tennessee Pass. After 1950 it was combined with the *Prospector* from Grand Junction to Salt Lake City. A bright spark appeared in 1956 when an agreement was reached with the Burlington for the *Royal Gorge* to carry cars from the *Denver Zephyr* between Denver and Colorado Springs, an arrangement which lasted until January 1, 1967. That portion of the run between Salida and Grand Junction was terminated on December 6, 1964, and the remainder of the train was finally discontinued on July 27, 1967.

Colorado Eagle (trains 3 and 4). On June 21, 1942, the Rio Grande and Missouri Pacific collaborated on a diesel-powered, streamlined train between St. Louis and Denver known as the *Colorado Eagle.* The train operated over the Joint Line between Pueblo and Denver with D&RGW crews but MOP equipment. Cut back to a shadow of its former grandeur, the *Colorado Eagle* was mercifully abandoned on May 16, 1966.

Prospector (trains 7 and 8). Conceived as the brainchild of D&RGW receiver Judge Wilson McCarthy in 1941, the original two-car *Prospector* supplied overnight service between Denver and Salt Lake City. The unconventional equipment was not successful, and the trains were withdrawn after only nine months on the road. Trains 7 and 8 were renamed the *Prospector* in October, 1945, and were the first Rio Grande trains to be dieselized just two years later. Sparkling new stainless steel cars were acquired for the train in 1950. In 1964, the *Prospector* became a kind of mixed train when up to four piggyback cars were added to the consist behind the pullman every night. This additional revenue did not prevent the trains from losing more money than all other D&RGW passenger trains combined, and the end came at last on May 28, 1967.

Yampa Valley Mail (trains 9 and 10). The beloved *Yampa Valley Mail* provided passenger service between Denver and Craig over the scenic Moffat Road commencing on September 5, 1954. Although "Mail" was officially dropped from the name during November, 1963, the train was still commonly known as the *Yampa Valley Mail.* The distinctive Alco PA-1 locomotives ran on trains 9 and 10 until they were traded to EMD for new freight power. The *Yampa Valley* made its last run reluctantly on April 7, 1968.

California Zephyr (trains 17 and 18). Born of an agreement among the Rio Grande, Burlington, and Western Pacific to offer elegant service between Chicago and San Francisco, the celebrated *California Zephyr* began its distinguished career on March 20, 1949. Heir to the *Exposition Flyer,* which had afforded service over the same route, the *California Zephyr* was immediately hailed as the greatest passenger train in North America. Recognition of the *CZ* as a mobile national monument did little to offset ever-increasing losses. On March 22, 1970, the destitute Western Pacific withdrew from the partnership and terminated its portion of the run. The Rio Grande and Burlington continued to operate the train three times a week between Chicago and Salt Lake City with a few cars continuing on to Ogden to connect with the Southern Pacific *City of San Francisco.* But the fabled *California Zephyr* died on March 22, 1970.

Rio Grande Zephyr (trains 17 and 18). When the *CZ* faded away, the D&RGW renamed its tri-weekly train between Denver and Salt Lake City the *Rio Grande Zephyr.* In 1971, at the last moment, the Rio Grande declined to join Amtrak and may be inclined to run the *RGZ* indefinitely to avoid the difficulties of handling Amtrak trains. The service remains superb, and the immaculate train is certainly one of the finest in the nation today.

Ski Train. In 1936 the Denver & Salt Lake started running the *Ski Train* between Denver and Hot Sulphur Springs. When the Winter Park ski area was developed in 1946, it became the destination of the ski specials, which were operated originally at the request of the Eskimo Ski Club. Today, every Saturday and Sunday during the ski season, the D&RGW still offers transportation to the ski slopes, a long-standing tradition on that line.

The *Royal Gorge,* train #2, zips through Englewood right on time. The last three cars were added in Colorado Springs and will go east to Chicago later that afternoon on the CB&Q *Denver Zephyr.* (3/21/65)

Powered by Alco PA-1 and PB-1 units, the *Royal Gorge* passes through Wolhurst on its last through run to Grand Junction. (12/5/64)

Time is running out for the *Royal Gorge*
as train #1 speeds along near Texas Creek.
(Photo by Ed Fulcomer, 5/7/67)

In a busier era, the westbound *Royal Gorge* is seen near Buena Vista with nine cars. Tennessee Pass lies ahead. (Photo by Howard Fogg)

Train #4, the eastbound *Colorado Eagle* crests the grade at Palmer Lake. The beautiful blue and cream streamliner is powered by two Alco PA-1's and an EMD E-7B. (Photo by Ross B. Grenard, 7/30/60)

The *Prospector* approaches Denver on a spring morning after an uneventful overnight run from Salt Lake City. During the last three years of the train's life, as many as four piggyback flat cars were added behind the pullman to generate additional revenue. (4/3/66)

The *Yampa Valley* is carrying an extra dome coach
as it nears Rocky on its westward run to Craig. (3/21/65)

Train #10, the *Yampa Valley,* pauses at Granby
to pick up a privately-owned business car.
(3/6/66)

Seen at Rock Creek Canyon above Bond, the eastbound *Yampa Valley* boasts an extra dome coach and business car for members of the Intermountain Chapter, National Railway Historical Society who were enjoying one of their legendary "last runs" to Craig. (3/6/66)

One of the most beloved of all D&RGW passenger trains, the *Yampa Valley* stops briefly at Steamboat Springs. Alas, discontinuance was less than one year away. (Photo by Ed Fulcomer, 4/29/67)

Inaugurated in 1949 to provide truly elegant service between Chicago and San Francisco over the Burlington, Rio Grande, and Western Pacific lines, the *California Zephyr* was immediately hailed as the foremost passenger train in the land. Here the celebrated *CZ* climbs westward toward tunnel #1. (3/27/65)

The *Yampa Valley* waits in the hole
for the passage of the *California Zephyr*
at Azure in Gore Canyon. (3/6/66)

Deep in the confines of Glenwood Canyon, the *California Zephyr* rolls along the Colorado River. The lead unit, F-9 #5771, was retained for use on the successor *Rio Grande Zephyr* and is today the only cab F-unit on the D&RGW roster. (Photo by Ed Fulcomer, 7/2/67)

When the Rio Grande declined to join Amtrak, the railroad was required to continue operation of a passenger train between Denver and Salt Lake City. The tri-weekly *Rio Grande Zephyr* was the result. It is viewed here as it departs from Denver Union Terminal. The second unit was converted from an Alco PB-1 to serve as a steam generator car, and the multiple-unit control lines pass through its body to reach the second F-9. (4/22/76)

Acclaimed today as the best
train in the country, the short
Rio Grande Zephyr assaults
the Front Range at tunnel #1.
(6/24/76)

Traversing some of the finest scenery in Colorado,
the *Rio Grande Zephyr* speeds westward between
Tolland and East Portal. (8/26/76)

The D&SL and later the D&RGW have run ski trains to the western slope during the winter months since 1936. Powered by two GP30's, the *Ski Train* pulls toward tunnel #1. (3/18/72)

Continuing a long-standing tradition of rail transportation to the ski slopes, a twenty-car *Ski Train* climbs through Plainview. (3/21/65)

The consist includes two dome coaches from the Denver mayor's party as the last *Ski Train* of the season rolls eastward through Winter Park after being turned on the wye at Tabernash. New GP40-2's provide the power. (3/29/75)

Photographic Data

Page	Camera	Lens	Film
Cover	Leica M-4	50mm Summicron f/2.0	Ilford Pan-F
Title Page	Hasselblad 500C/M	80mm Planar f/2.8	Ilford FP-4
5	Leica M-3	50mm Summicron f/2.0	Agfa IF
6	Rolleiflex	75mm Tessar f/3.5	Ilford FP-4
7	Leica M-4	200mm Telyt f/4.0	Ilford Pan-F
8 (both)	Leica M-4	200mm Telyt f/4.0	Ilford Pan-F
9	Rolleiflex	75mm Tessar f/3.5	Ilford Pan-F
10 (both)	Leica M-4	200mm Telyt f/4.0	Ilford Pan-F
11	Leica M-4	50mm Summicron f/2.0	Agfapan 25
12	Rolleiflex	75mm Tessar f/3.5	Ilford FP-4
13	Hasselblad 500C/M	80mm Planar f/2.8	EFKE R-14
14	Leica M-4	50mm Summicron f/2.0	Agfapan 25
15	Hasselblad 500C/M	80mm Planar f/2.8	EFKE R-14
16	Leica M-4	50mm Summicron f/2.0	Agfapan 25
17	Rolleiflex	75mm Tessar f/3.5	Ilford FP-4
18	Hasselblad 500C/M	80mm Planar f/2.8	EFKE R-14
20	Rolleiflex	75mm Tessar f/3.5	Ilford FP-4
21	Nikon F	105mm Nikkor f/2.5	Ilford Pan-F
22	Rolleiflex	75mm Tessar f/3.5	Ilford FP-4
23	Rolleiflex	75mm Tessar f/3.5	Ilford FP-4
24	Rolleiflex	75mm Tessar f/3.5	Ilford FP-4
25	Rolleiflex	75mm Tessar f/3.5	Ilford Pan-F
26	Rolleiflex	75mm Tessar f/3.5	Ilford FP-4
27	Kodak Medalist	Ektar f/3.5	Tri-X
28	Rolleiflex	75mm Tessar f/3.5	Ilford FP-4
29	Rolleiflex	75mm Tessar f/3.5	Ilford FP-4
30	Leica M-4	50mm Summicron f/2.0	Ilford Pan-F
31	Nikon F	105mm Nikkor f/2.5	Ilford Pan-F
32	Rolleiflex	75mm Tessar f/3.5	Ilford FP-4
33	Rolleiflex	75mm Tessar f/3.5	Ilford FP-4
34	Nikon F	105mm Nikkor f/2.5	Ilford Pan-F
35	Rolleiflex	75mm Tessar f/3.5	Ilford FP-4
36	Leica M-4	50mm Summicron f/2.0	Ilford Pan-F
37	Rolleiflex	75mm Tessar f/3.5	Ilford FP-4
38	Leica M-3	50mm Summicron f/2.0	Ektachrome-X

Page	Camera	Lens	Film
40	Leica M-4	50mm Summicron f/2.0	Agfapan 25
41	Leica M-3	200mm Telyt f/4.0	Plus-X
42	Nikon F	105mm Nikkor f/2.5	Adox KB-17
43	Nikon F	105mm Nikkor f/2.5	Ilford Pan-F
44	Nikon F	105mm Nikkor f/2.5	Ilford Pan-F
45	Rolleiflex	75mm Tessar f/3.5	Agfapan 25
46	Rolleiflex	75mm Tessar f/3.5	Plus-X
47	Leica M-4	50mm Summicron f/2.0	Agfapan 25
48	Rolleiflex	75mm Tessar f/3.5	Agfapan 25
49	Rolleiflex	75mm Tessar f/3.5	Agfapan 25
50	Hasselblad 500C/M	80mm Planar f/2.8	Ilford FP-4
51	Rolleiflex	75mm Tessar f/3.5	Ilford FP-4
52	Nikon F	105mm Nikkor f/2.5	Ilford Pan-F
53	Leica M-4	50mm Summicron f/2.0	Agfapan 25
54	Nikon F	105mm Nikkor f/2.5	Adox KB-17
55	Leica M-4	50mm Summicron f/2.0	Ilford Pan-F
56	Leica M-4	50mm Summicron f/2.0	Ilford FP-4
57	Leica M-3	50mm Summicron f/2.0	Plus-X
58	Yashica D	Unknown	Plus-X
60	Leica M-3	200mm Telyt f/4.0	Plus-X
61	Leica M-3	50mm Summicron f/2.0	Adox KB-14
62	Kodak Medalist	Ektar f/3.5	Tri-X
63	Ciro-Flex	85mm Anastigmat f/3.5	Verichrome Professional
64	Data Not Available		
65	Leica M-2	90mm Elmarit f/2.8	Agfachrome
66	Leica M-3	200mm Telyt f/4.0	Plus-X
67	Leica M-3	50mm Summicron f/2.0	Plus-X
68	Leica M-3	50mm Summicron f/2.0	Plus-X
69	Kodak Medalist	Ektar f/3.5	Verichrome Pan
70	Leica M-3	90mm Elmarit f/2.8	Plus-X
71	Leica M-3	50mm Summicron f/2.0	Plus-X
72	Kodak Medalist	Ektar f/3.5	Tri-X
73	Rolleiflex	75mm Tessar f/3.5	Ilford Pan-F
74	Rolleiflex	75mm Tessar f/3.5	Plus-X
75	Rolleiflex	75mm Tessar f/3.5	Ilford FP-4
76	Nikon F	105mm Nikkor f/2.5	Ilford Pan-F
77	Leica M-3	200mm Telyt f/4.0	Plus-X
78	Leica M-4	50mm Summicron f/2.0	Ilford FP-4